Janice Jordan

Barbra
give always
w/no expectations
a great Richley
Janice Jordan

It's more than Wine and Meatballs

Janice Jordan

Janice Jordan

DEDICATION

I dedicate this book to Mary Purvis, who took my hand at that very first networking event and introduced me to every person in the room. That day, I knew I had to do the same and help other people get over their discomfort and learn to grow through networking. Also, to my loving husband, Michael and great friends and family.

Janice Jordan

CONTENTS

Janice Jordan

ACKNOWLEDGMENTS

I would like to thank
- Joel Canfield for telling me I had a book in me and needed to write it.
- My husband, Michael, for supporting me.
- Mary Pervis for introducing me to all the people in the room at that first networking event.
- Robert Welton for his input on the chamber of commerce information.
- The Chamber of Commerce and networking groups like BNI®, TNI® and LeTip® for letting me learn all I can about how it works so I can share how to get the most out these lead groups.
- All the people over the years with whom I have networked, learned from and taught. Thank you for letting me share your stories.

Janice Jordan

Chapter 1

Introduction to Networking

Networking Tip: It's about building relationships and doing business with people you know, like and trust.

Networking Tip: Make networking part of your marketing plan.

Networking Tip: Some people find networking difficult because it is not what we were taught in marketing class. Time to think outside the box.

Chapter 1

Introduction to Networking

I started networking many years ago — before networking was cool. I worked for corporate America and had to prove to management that networking was a better way to grow my territory than cold calling. I convinced them by learning everything I could about networking organizations and chambers and then by becoming a top sales representative. I grew my territory by relationship building through networking. At first, I had to pay for chamber of commerce memberships out of pocket. Eventually, management saw the benefit and paid for my memberships. What I want to share with you is where my passion for networking came from and how I came to the decision to write this book for you.

A few years ago, I was fired from my job because of office politics. I was in my mid-40s. I found myself single and unemployed. Surviving and paying my bills were my sole concerns. I no longer wanted to work for someone else and be vulnerable to losing everything again. I didn't know what to do. I told a friend, "If I could make a living networking, I would be very happy and very good at it." She suggested I conduct a round table. This is where a group of people discuss and share ideas on a subject. I put it out to my network that I needed some help. Nine entrepreneurs joined me to help strategize my business plan. They gave two hours of their time and paid for their own lunch. They showed up with contracts and business plans and brainstorming ideas. It was so exciting! What an awesome feeling that these nine people thought so much of me to give me their time and ideas. That's how Referral Network was formed. These were people I knew from networking and I had helped them in the past. Now they all helped me. That's what networking is all about — helping others. When you give a referral, it comes back to you five fold. In my case nine fold! My business was built by networking, and still grows through networking. You can grow *yours* through networking too.

I am passionate about networking because I know first-hand that it works. When you build your business and your life by building relationships, you have a very full existence, great friends, great clients and great customers who continue to grow with you.

Networking isn't new. It's been around for a long time. Go back to the gold rush days when people were moving west and growing the country. Towns grew through the art of networking. We just had a different name for it back then — we called it being *neighborly*. Think about it. The general store was the central location where the women would talk while shopping and share receipts and patterns. The men would talk about hunting and farming. As people got to know each other, if someone needed something the whole town chipped in. The church was another source. After services, the congregation held social events, picnics and dances. As the towns and communities grew, there were more places to network. These became the chambers of commerce and organizations we know today.

I hope this book shows you how to network more effectively to make your business and life full. I never thought I would write a book. But a very smart man I met through networking told me I would. He is an author and speaks on the subject that every entrepreneur has a book inside of themselves. I didn't believe I could, but he insisted that I please try. He said that I have more information and knowledge about networking than anyone he knows and it needed to be written. So here is the book my friend said I should write and I hope it serves as a great tool to you. I want you to feel the passion I have and success I have by having friends and customers in your life. This is my way to pay it forward. Please enjoy this book and pass it on to others.

Chapter 2

Where to Network

Networking Tip: Choose a chamber of commerce where you work or live.

Networking Tip: When joining a Leads group, you want to have a *warm fuzzy* feeling about it. You will be meeting with this group once a week.

Chapter 2

Where to Network

There are many choices of where to network. It can take months and a lot of money to find out which is the best place to spend your time to get the clients you want. Here are a few places to choose from and what to look for when making your choice. Research all groups and chambers of commerce online before joining. Attend the organization in which you are interested at least twice and ask a lot of questions before joining. You want to have a warm and fuzzy feeling (trust comfort level) about the group or organization you are joining. This could be a one-year commitment or more. Use the three/three rule. There must be three people or business categories that fit your ideal client profile that you can do business with or refer to. There also must be three people or business types that want your services or products and can refer you. Let's look at the choices.

There are Two Types of Chamber of Commerce.

1. *Regional chambers* **of commerce** cover multiple regions and focus on business. They work with the government to pass laws on behalf of small to large businesses. Some of the services regional chambers of commerce provide for businesses include (but not limited to):

   - Free business plans
   - Discounted health plans
   - Networking events
   - Advice and ideas for growing business
   - Business connections

2. **Local chambers** focus on local government and community. Join your local chamber and get involved in your community — this is a great tool for any small business. Join the chamber near where you live or work. Members include

individuals, entrepreneurs, small to medium size businesses and a few large businesses. You'll find members do business with other members. They offer great services, too. Check your local chamber of commerce to see what benefits its membership brings.

How to Use Regional and Local Chambers

- Attend regularly.
- Go to all networking events and bring business cards, flyers and a raffle prize (when applicable).
- Join a committee that relates to your business. For example, if your business is related to education you may want to be on the education committee.
- Join a committee like the ambassadors to meet new members and work with long-time members too.

Associations are forums of industry-specific or like-minded people. While you may not receive many referrals from associations, they are helpful with business issues. They provide a way to band together with people like you and to grow and learn from others. They facilitate the sharing of ideas and what works and what doesn't. They Save you time and money. One well-known example is National Association of Realtors®.

How to Use Associations

- Attend regularly.
- Ask questions.
- Share ideas.
- Get involved and participate in group functions.

Lead Source Groups mainly generate leads or referrals. BNI®, TNI® and LeTip® are three known leads groups and you can find many small, local groups. Leads groups are industry exclusive — only one person per business category. You share referrals among the group. It's like having your own little sales force. You help grow their businesses as they help grow yours. You need to work at having qualified referrals and bring guests to keep the group growing and fresh.

What to look for in a group:

- Located conveniently in your area close to work or home.

- Fits your schedule and meets for breakfast or lunch.

- Ideally, it should have 20 to 40 members. Start-up groups may have fewer–hopefully more than 10 members. (note: when you join a start-up, you also spend time building the group.)

- Aim for at least three members with whom you can exchange referrals. These are your power partners. It would be great if you are able to give and get referrals from everyone in the group, but it usually doesn't work that way. So if you can give and get referrals from three people steadily, the group will be able to grow.

- It's important that you connect with a group that gives you what I call a *warm fuzzy* — people you know, like and trust. Leads groups require a one-year commitment and meet weekly for about one and half hours. It helps if you like the members!

- It also helps to be proactive and try to get to know each member quickly. The better you get to know each other, the more chances for referrals and for doing business together. The way to do this is with one-on-one meetings with the members of these groups in between the regularly scheduled meetings.

Belonging to a leads group is like having your own sales force. It puts you in front of the people who will be your clients. You pay for this service by doing the same for them. The more you give, the more you get back. I recommend you go through the chairs and be part of the leadership team.

Some leads group business types include:

- Finance
- Real estate
- Hair dresser
- Service related

Meet-up and Mastermind Groups. These are online businesses and social groups in your area. They are great resources for like-minded business people and great for referring service. Find a group with 10 or more members who give you that *warm fuzzy* — people you can grow to know, like and trust.

Business types participating in these groups include multi-level marketing (MLMs), direct sellers, small businesses and more.

How to Use Meet-up and Mastermind Groups

- Attend regularly.
- Get involved.
- Share and be open. Ask questions and give back to the group.

Social Networking. This is online networking with sites like Facebook®, Twitter®, and LinkedIn®. Social networking is a good way to stay connected or start a connection, however face-to–face is still important. You need to do both and they work hand in hand. If

ance Jordan

you meet people online, at some point you should meet face to face in order to build a relationship. If you meet face to face, then online is a great way to stay in contact and keep your name and face in front of your prospect. The object is to build a relationship in which you and your contact know, like and trust each other.

We could do a whole book on social networking. I am not even going to do a chapter. There are many experts in this field. I am not one of them. I use social networking a lot to grow and maintain my business. My expertise is with the face-to-face networking which is, in my opinion, a major part of marketing and growing your business. It works hand in hand with network marketing and is a great referral source.

Service Organizations primarily function to give back to the community. Volunteers organize community awareness and hold fundraisers for those in need. While this kind of group is not ideal as a referral source, (but can be a referral source) belonging to a service organization is a great way to do your part for the community. Well-known examples of service organizations include Kiwanis®, Rotary® and Lions®.

Toastmasters® is a non-profit international organization that offers a way to practice and hone your communication and leadership skills. Members typically meet weekly. Look for a group with 15 or more members who meet on a day, location and time convenient for your schedule. Members practice prepared and impromptu speeches and the other members critique them on timing, delivery, grammar and more. These groups are not typical networking groups, however they help you improve the skills you need to become successful. In the process, members learn more about each other.

Toastmasters members include anyone wanting to improve his or her communication skills.

There is no shortage of networking organizations from which to choose. Now that you know a bit about chambers of commerce, associations, leads groups, meet-ups and masterminds, social networking, service organizations and Toastmasters, you can make your choice. The skills and tools in this book can help you decide which of these groups work for you. How you choose may also depend on your personality and individual needs. I highly recommend you look them up online and let your fingers do the walking before you join any organization. Feel free to try out different groups until you find the right fit for you. Join one or a select few — if you get involved in too many, you will not have time to work your business.

In Review: Check out each group before joining.

- Research on line.

- Visit at least twice. Ask questions.

- They need to fit your schedule, and location.

- Have a warm fuzzy

- Size of the group

- The three/three rule – at least three people you can refer to and get referrals from. Three people who can use your service and refer you.

- Do your homework on the group and when you join be present and proactive.

Chapter 3

Get Into the Swing of Networking

Networking Tip: Prepare for the event. Make a plan and set a goal.

Networking Tip: Always be on time or show up early to greet new attendees and network.

Networking Tip: Treat every event like it's an appointment.

Chapter 3

Get into the Swing of Networking

Networking is like a golf swing. Imagine yourself on the golf course. You just arrived at the first tee. As you get out of the cart, you must decide which club to use. Just closing your eyes and picking one isn't the best way to play the game. In order to pick the right club, you must know the hole. Know the distance to the hole, if there are water or sand traps and which way the wind is blowing. The same thing pertains to networking. You can go to a networking event blindly, not knowing who will be there and unprepared. On the other hand, you can know the room and come with the right tools. By having a plan and a goal, you can play your best game.

Do a little homework prior to the event. The more you know about the group or chamber of commerce and who will be there, the better your chances of getting in front of the people you need to talk to. Check the RSVP list online.

Ask a friend who is a member about the meeting format and what businesses attend. Is it a sit down? A mixer? Formal or informal?

Now that you have your club of choice, you are ready to hit the ball. Do you just walk up to the tee, hit the ball, hope it's a good shot and get back in the cart? Not quite. If golf were that easy, everyone would play and the pros wouldn't need to practice every day. You need to line up to the ball and get ready to swing. Remember the steps and do them with exact precision: head down, arms straight, knees bent, feet apart, head down, eyes on the ball, back straight, bottom out, chin up and head down. Then swing and hit the ball on the exact spot and follow through while continuing the steps in the swing. Again, the same applies to networking. You could just walk in, socialize, pick up a few business cards and call it networking. However, to be a pro you need to do more. When you approach someone, it's important to:

- reach out to shake their hand
- make eye contact
- smile
- listen
- talk
- think about who you can refer them to
- think about what your next question will be
- continue smiling, listening and talking!
- look around the room
- keep it short
- know your product
- know your introduction
- continue smiling, listening and talking!
- have fun
- move on to the next person

These are steps you must take to be a great networker. As you can see, you must do more than one thing at a time — and don't forget to smile, listen, talk, and have fun!

All of this and you haven't even hit the ball yet. You just entered the room and you still have the whole event ahead of you, plus the follow up.

In golf, it's important to swing through, keep momentum and follow through. Bring your arms and the club all the way around. If you don't, the ball goes nowhere and you might as well be playing croquet. The same goes with networking. The follow-up is the most important part of networking. Without it, you're just socializing and it's just *wine and meatballs*.

When you swing, you must remember the other steps and hit through the ball. While networking, you need to decide if you want to get to know this person better. If so, do not lose your momentum. Offer your business card and plan to follow up. If you decide not to take it to the next step, politely move on to network with other people. Everyone you meet is not your perfect match. You may not have enough information to decide that yet. You may see someone every month for several events before you both have that *warm fuzzy*. That's okay. It's part of building a relationship and getting to know, like and trust someone. Remember to keep moving — be considerate of people's time and don't hold up the game.

Ask open-ended questions to find out if someone is a good fit for you or a good referral source. In a game of golf, you may hit the ball many times to play all 18 holes. As you play more and learn the course, it takes fewer swings and less time to play the game. In networking, it may require making many contacts to connect with a few clients. As you practice and get to know the people and the room, it becomes easier.

As in golf, there is a learning curve in networking. The more you work at it, the better and more effective you become. Many pros have mentors or coaches. I recommend you connect with a mentor or coach as well.

In golf, you need to know the course, have the proper clubs and balls, know how to use them and practice, practice, practice. You must have good follow through and have fun and passion playing the game. In networking, you need to know the room — the group, the organization, the chamber of commerce. Come prepared with the right tools, such as business cards and flyers, and come with the appropriate skills. Know your introduction and product with passion, communicate and follow up, follow up, follow up. Have fun and play the game!

In Review: Networking is like golf. You need to have the right tools, skills, passion, a strong work ethic and practice. The important part of golf is the follow through the important part of networking is the follow-up.

Chapter 4

Three Key Strategies to Better Networking

Networking Tip: Be the best you can be, be present to win and don't except anything less.

Networking Tip: Be positive, passionate, focused and have fun.

Networking Tip: Invite a friend to go to a networking event with you.

Chapter 4

Three Key Strategies for Better Networking

In Chapter 3 we focused on networking skills. Every game has both skill and strategy — and so does networking. In this chapter we will work on strategy. Many people think that all they need to do is show up and visit, and call that networking. However, networking is much more than that. To network with success, I encourage you to have a strategy — to plan what, where and how to play the game.

Implement these Three Strategies

1. Be prepared

2. Formulate a plan

3. Set your goals

Be prepared. This means more than just showing up with business cards in hand. Treat every event as an appointment. When you schedule it in your calendar,

keep the appointment. Be present and consistent —
or your competition may pick up where you left off!

Just as you would prepare for a sales appointment,
you should prepare for a networking event. In
preparation for a sales meeting, you might research
the company to learn what service or product would
fit its needs. How many employees work there? What
service or product does the company offer? You
would also have the appropriate tools you need to
present to your contact.

Savvy networkers prepare this way for events. Go on
a fact finding mission to learn what attendees need.
The more you know about the organization, group or
chamber event you attend, the better chance you
have to get in front of the people you want to meet.
People you know can introduce you to people you
don't know.

Knowing who will be there helps you chose the right
tools to bring. Do your research. Check the RSVP list
to know who will be in the room. If you want to meet
realtors, look for names that are familiar in the real
estate world. Look them up on Facebook® or
Linkedin® to see what they look like and find
information about their businesses. Then when you
meet them at the event, you will have warm leads
instead of cold ones.

Formulate a plan. Planning and organization are essential tools in networking. When you take a vacation you have a plan. When you get married you have a plan. When you look for a job you have a plan. When you attend a networking event you need a plan, too. As a business owner, your marketing plan should include networking. Your networking plan includes what you need to accomplish yearly, quarterly, monthly, weekly — and even what you want to accomplish at each event.

Plan what tools you need for each event. For example:

- business cards

- flyers

- a good, practiced and adaptable introduction

- a raffle prize

- knowledge of your products or services

- which product or service you want to share at this event

Make a plan and stick to it. Golfers plan every move to get the ball closer to the hole. The same thing applies to networking.

Set your goals. Goal setting is crucial in life, in business and in networking. Set a goal for every networking event. Your goal should be reachable, written and spoken, trackable and date or time sensitive. A goal also gives you purpose and keeps you focused.

Your event goal might be:

- To meet five new people

- to introduce two people to someone else in the room

- To meet one person who likes dogs

Share your goal with others. If people know your goal, they can help you fulfill it. You can share your goal with the event ambassadors, greeters or even the host. Their roles are to introduce and connect people and to encourage the *warm fuzzy*. If you tell them that you need to meet realtors, chiropractors or landscapers, they may be able to find that match for you. Also, share your goal with the people handling the registration table. They know everyone who checks in and they have a list of their names and businesses.

I would like to share a very special story about an awesome ambassador who knew my goal and helped me make a valuable connection.

I attended a local chamber luncheon in December. As I walked in through the door, an ambassador I knew was one of the greeters. She knew I always had the same goal: to meet 5 new people. She said she had someone for me to meet who was new to the city and to the chamber. This was his first event and he knew very few people. She gave me his card and filled me in on a few details about him and his business. I thanked her and headed in to find him and introduce myself.

I still had not found him when it was time to be seated for lunch. As I approached the table, I saw a young man I didn't know. His name tag had "new Member" on it. I knew immediately this was the person the ambassador wanted me to meet. It was the Christmas season and I decided to have a little fun. I walked straight up to him like I already knew him well. I shook his hand and said, "Wow! You must be _____. It's so great to meet you. I understand you joined the chamber today and just moved here from _____. He was so surprised, he didn't know what to say. He asked me how I knew all this. I said, "So, you sell _____? What can you tell me about it?" I continued the game and didn't tell him how I knew all about him. He didn't have a clue who I was. The ambassador who gave me the information was sitting at the same table and went right along with me. When he asked me again how I knew all this about him, I explained that I had "Santa Clause syndrome." I told him that I knew who was naughty or nice and that he was a very good boy." My ambassador friend struggled not to laugh. By the end of lunch, we had set up a coffee meeting. He gave me a hug and shook the ambassador's hand. I had so much fun that day and he was such a good sport.

At the coffee meeting, I explained to him how I knew about him. We have become great friends and have a great business relationship. He took my coaching class and grew his business quickly. And the relationship between he and the ambassador has also grown. She and I continue to share goals and referrals.

The moral of the story is to have a goal and share it with others — and have some fun!

Put these three key strategies into action. Be prepared, formulate a plan and set your goals. You'll learn about two additional key strategies in the following chapters about follow-through and referrals.

In Review: Remember — prepare like it's an appointment, know who is in the room and have the proper tools. Have a plan and stick to it. Stay focused. Finally, set doable goals and share them with others.

It's More than Wine and Meatballs

Chapter 5

The 6 Characters of Networking

Networking Tip: Do not pass out business cards to everyone in the room. Get to know who you are talking to and then only give or receive requested cards.

Networking Tip: Just because someone has an email address on his or her business card does not give you permission to put that person on a mailing list.

Chapter 5

The Six Characters of Networking

We sometimes pick up bad habits from watching what others do because we don't know what we don't know. I call these habits *characters*, because people tend to take on these roles like characters in a story. In this chapter, I will go over these characters and share with you how to turn them around into something positive. Most of us have displayed one or more of these at some point. When someone you know acts like one of these characters, you can politely point it out and share with them the best way to change it.

1. **The Card Player.** You may have seen this person. He hands out business cards to everyone he sees and wants everyone else's

card in return. It's as if he is in a contest to see how many cards he can collect — or in a card game trying to get that royal flush.

When you acquire cards this way, what do you do with them? You have not made any real connections with these people before contacting them. You are still cold calling. You might as well go to a business card kiosk at your local auto repair shop, pull all the cards and call them. They don't know you, therefore this would not be effective. You also end up with a lot of business cards — too many to follow up on. It's easier to follow up on 5 contacts you spoke with at an event than with 30 random business cards of people you never met.

Instead of being the Card Player, become the *Card Shark*. Only give your business card to those who ask for it. Then give them two cards — one to keep and one to pass on for a referral. Only ask for a card from someone you have met and who is of interest to you, to your business or to someone you know. This way, you walk away with precious few business cards — ones that will be easier to follow up on because you know each other. It becomes a warm call instead of a cold one.

2, **The Magician.** Is a cardplayer who touches her magic wand to your business card and turns it into an unsolicited newsletter that appears in your inbox once a week. This gives the impression she is trying to sell to you before earning the right. Plus, unsolicited email is spam, is illegal and may result in the sender getting fined.

If you identify with *The Magician*, you can turn this around by simply asking for permission to put someone on your email list. Just because an email address is on someone's business card doesn't give you permission to put that person on a mailing list. You can send a short, *Glad I met you* email within 24 hours — one that is not salesy. If you don't receive a response, you do not have permission to put that person on your list. Follow up by phone or in person. You can also use an email system that has a permission and opt-out option.

2. **The Badge Gazer.** This person only looks for people in certain professions at networking events. If you don't fit his ideal client profile, he does not want to talk to you. I am always amazed when I see *The Badge Gazer* hurrying by everyone, bent over and reading name

badges. This person is in a hurry to talk only to people he thinks he can sell to. He believes his time is more important than yours. He typically shows up late, finds one or two people to exchange cards with him and then leaves early.

If you find yourself in the role of *The Badge Gazer*, you are doing yourself — not to mention others — a disservice. Turn this around by simply treating people with kindness and respect. Chances are they are more likely to bring their business to you. Treat an event as an appointment. Give it the same attention and focus you would for a million dollar client.

There are no short cuts in life. Make a plan and be present to win. Show up and do the work necessary to build relationships. Know in advance who will be in the room in order to meet the people you want to quickly and efficiently — and without being rude. With the help of the RSVP list, ambassadors and the registration table, find out who you know, who you don't know and who can introduce you to quality connections. You never know who has the Verizon network behind them, so talk to as many people as possible whether you believe they are your clients or not. We instinctively want to sell and this is a difficult character to avoid becoming. However with practice, you can turn this around into a more positive approach for networking success.

3. **The Closer**. This person not only tries to sell — she actually pounces on you to buy *now*. No one likes being the victim of the closer. *Closers like to pounce.* She is the first to say that networking doesn't work. Why? Because she doesn't close any sales at networking events.

Here is an example of why *A Closer* does not succeed at networking. I was at an event one evening and overheard a conversation between a *Closer* and a friend of mine. He introduced himself, handed my friend a card and proceeded to talk about his product. My friend politely thanked him and said, "I don't have a need for that service." *The Closer* said, "That's okay, then I have this card for you." He pulled out another card and pounced again. My friend was amazed and politely said, "Thank you. I will consider the information." Unbelievably, he said, "Well, I am sure you have to need this service, everyone does." He handed my friend yet another business card.

The *Closer* never asked my friend questions or tried to make a personal connection. All three of his business cards were thrown in the trash. Because he didn't have my friend's business card, he also could not follow up.

Avoiding the role of *The Closer* is simple. Realize that it's not about you. Sales training may have taught you to be aggressive and that it's all about you. You may have been conditioned to sell, sell, sell and to look at the numbers. In networking however, nobody likes to be sold to. Effective networkers educate people without selling to them. Introduce yourself and explain what you do — while being respectful of them and their time. You may set an appointment outside of the event to give a presentation — and that is where you can do the selling. But even then, do it kindly. Don't be pushy or salesy. Build the relationship and ask for the order. ***ASK*** – **A**lways **S**ell **K**indly.

4. **The Town Crier.** This person is the life of the party. He knows about everything and flutters about loudly. He behaves as if the whole event was put on just for him and thinks everyone there wants to know only him. He seems to think his product is the best and that it will even help yours look good. He never gives you a chance to talk.

You can avoid behaving like *The Town Crier* by listening more and talking less. We have two ears and one mouth for a reason. Again, realize it's not about you. Don't try so hard for people to like you. If you simply be yourself, they will.

5. **The Crasher.** This is the person at a networking event who is so excited to see you that she interrupts your conversation, cutting off the person you are already talking to. Like the Town Crier, *The Crasher* does not seem to realize that all the attendees are not all there just to see her. The Crasher may not realize she is being rude. She sees someone she knows and gets excited. She behaves as if her time is more important than yours. You may have walked away from this interruption unhappy and remember her as being rude.

Have you been *The Crasher*? This behavior could cause you to lose your next $10,000 client. Again, understand that it's not all about you — networking is about everyone else. Make every effort to avoid interrupting people who are in conversation. Give them plenty of room and wait patiently for them to invite you into their conversation. If they don't do so quickly, you may want to move on and try to get back to them when they are finished. You only have a couple of hours to get in front of as many people you can.

I remember an experience I had with someone who combined several of these characters of networking into one.

At a chamber mixer, *I was in a conversation with someone I had just met. A woman ran up to us. She was in a hurry. "There is only five minutes left and I haven't given everyone my card," she said. "I need to get yours too, so I can put you on my mailing list so you can get the latest updates in real estate." I looked at her in disbelief and at the card she had pushed into my hand. She had no idea who we were or what we did. She didn't care. All she wanted was our business cards to put into her data base. The person I was talking to handed her his card as a reflex. She informed him that he'd be getting an email from her tomorrow. She then looked at me for my card. I said, "I get a few real estate newsletters already. Thank you, but I just couldn't get another one." She responded, "You didn't give me your card anyway." She walked to the next group of people and repeated what she had done with us. While she was collecting cards from them, she said, "I just met the rudest woman. She didn't give me her card," and pointed to me. They told her that I was the queen of networking and very nice. They suggested she check me out online and take one of my workshops.*

She was a crasher, a card player and a magician. She didn't know any better. After watching other people, she probably thought she was being more efficient by getting a lot of cards and putting them on her mailing list. Instead, all she had was a large stack of meaningless business cards. She had not taken the time to get to know them. The moral of the story is there is no fast way or shortcuts. Networking is do the <u>work</u> and <u>net </u>the rewards.

In review: Remember the six characters of networking and what you can do instead.

1. **The Card Player** passes business cards to and receives business cards from everyone. Instead, only give and receive requested cards — and only when you have talked with the person.
2. **The Magician** adds people to his or her mailing list without their permission. Instead, ask permission to email and get to know people first.
3. **The Badge Gazer** reads badges and only talks to people in a certain industry. Instead, meet everyone, regardless of their industry. You don't know who may have the Verizon network

behind them, and can introduce you to the person who becomes your next big client.

4. **The Closer** pounces on you and tries to sell at events. Instead, know the importance of a good introduction. Educate people without selling to them. Remember that it's not about you and that the selling takes place at a later time.

5. **The Town Crier** talks all about himself, wanting to be the center of attention. He has the best product or service there is and knows everything and then some. Instead, listen and share. Be honest, have integrity and be sincere.

6. **The Crasher** interrupts conversations. *Instead,* wait to be invited into the conversation.

Just be *you*, have fun and ASK – always sell kindly.

Chapter 6

Your Adaptable Introduction

Networking Tip: Make sure your networking tool box contains the most important thing — a good introduction.

Networking Tip: Know your introduction and practice it daily.

Networking Tip: Infuse your introduction with passion and humor, and be sure it comes from your heart.

Chapter 6

Adaptable Introduction

One of the most important tools for networking is your introduction. Some people call this a commercial or elevator pitch, which makes you think of sales. However, your introduction leads to relationship building, therefore it should not be salesy or canned. It should be honest, passionate, practiced and polished. It needs to come from your heart. I call it an *adaptable introduction* because it should be adaptable in length and sometimes in content, depending on the person or persons to whom you are talking.

In this chapter, you will learn how to make an introduction that is 7 to 60 seconds long. Why is a good, adaptable introduction important? You may already know that *you only get one chance to make a good first impression*. You may also have heard that *luck is where preparedness meets opportunity*. What I really want to emphasize here is that an adaptable introduction is your most important tool in your networking tool bag. He who learns his skill and has the best tools, builds the best widget. To be skilled, you must practice, practice, practice. Again, as in golf, the pros practice often.

With everything else you need to know to run your business, you don't want to memorize a bunch of different introductions. I am going to show you how to use key words to trigger the memory portion of your brain and create many introductions. There are many studies that show we can remember up to seven things at a time. We are going to use 7 as our starting point and make a 7-second introduction that is adaptable to 60 seconds.

The following is an exercise to build your adaptable introduction.

Step 1. Keywords. You should be using the same keywords in all your marketing materials — from your website to your business cards to your printed brochures. These keywords describe your business. They are the words your clients use to find you. Use these same keywords to create your adaptable introduction.

<u>Keywords for a 60-second introduction</u>

If you had to describe your business in just one word, what would it be?

Describe your business in one word (try to think of six different one-word descriptions):

For example, if you are a networking coach, your keywords might be: Trainer, Coach, Teacher, Networking and Marketing

_____   _____   _____

_____   _____   _____

Now use these keywords to create phrases that describe what you do.

Describe your business in three-word phrases:

_____   _____   _____

_____   _____   _____

_____   _____   _____

For example, network more effectively

When people ask you what you do, what do you tell them? If you tell them what you sell, what kind of reaction do you get? Do they run away? Instead, give them a short, descriptive answer that makes them want to know more about you—not wonder what it is that you do. Don't make them play 50 Questions to find out what you do. Be honest and passionate about what you do. This gives off positive energy.

Remember that our brains can remember seven items at a time. Make a sentence that is no longer than seven words. This will be your seven-second introduction. This sentence triggers the memory section of your brain to just flow without having to memorize a long introduction.
Describe your business in a seven-word sentence:

_____ _____ _____

_____ _____ _____

_____

For example, I teach people more effective networking techniques.
Now you have your keywords and a seven-second introduction.

Step 2. The 60-second Adaptable introduction:
Create a 60-second adaptable introduction. A good introduction is made up of 5 parts.

1. The introduction. Include your name and business name.

2. The summary. Describe your product or service and what's in it for them (WIFM).

3. Your needs. Tell what you are looking for, your target market, about you.

4. Call to action. Give them something to do, like *Visit my website* or *Call me*.

5. Memorable tag line or hook. End with something to remember you by. This may be a good place for humor.

Use the keywords you listed to create your 60-second adaptable introduction. Enter a keyword next to each part below and use that keyword in your descriptions.

60-Second Introduction

Introduction _____

_____

Example: My name is _____ *and I am with*

_____*.*

Summary of product/service (WIFM) _____

_____

_____

_____

Example: I offer coaching and workshops to show
you how to network.

Your needs, target market, about you _____

_____

_____

_____

Example: *I teach you to be more effective at*
networking

Call to action _____

_____

_____

Example: Please check out my workshop schedule
on my website.

Memorable tag line, hook _____

_____

_____

Example: I help you grow through referrals

Simply combine the five parts to create your adaptable introduction. This is where you can have some fun and be creative. The five parts do not have to be in order. You can place the introduction in the beginning, in the middle or at the end. You can make your summary in the form of a question and place it at the beginning. Relax be yourself have fun. Combine the five parts here to create your 60-second Introduction:_____

_____

_____

_____

_____

_____

_____

_____

_____

Example: Would you like to come out of a networking event with 5 contacts instead of 30 business cards? I am Janice Jordan of Jordan's Referral Network and I teach you how to be more effective at networking through my coaching classes and workshops. Please check out my workshop schedule on my website. Let me show you how to grow in networking and referrals.

You may want to play with this a few different ways. Practice it until it is comfortable and in your own words.

Your introduction needs to be perfect. It's your first impression and sets you apart from everyone else. It sets you up as the expert and is the beginning to a business relationship. I suggest you do this exercise more than once. Below is the exercise we discussed:

Practice Page

Describe your business in one word.

_____ _____ _____

_____ _____ _____

Describe your business a in three-word phrase.

_____ _____ _____

_____ _____ _____

_____ _____ _____

Describe your business in a seven-word sentence.

_____ _____ _____

_____ _____ _____ _____

60-Second Introduction

Introduction _____

_____

Summary of product/service (WIFM) _____

_____

_____

Your needs, target market, about you _____

_____

_____

_____

Call to action

_____

_____

_____

Memorable tag line, hook _____

_____

_____

_____

60-Second Introduction (combine the five parts to create your introduction)

_____

_____

_____

_____

_____

_____

_____

_____

_____

_____

In Review: *The introduction is a significant part of networking. By making it adaptable, you have your 7-second introduction that opens up the lines of communication and your 30-60 second introduction that tells your story. It has 5 parts: introduction, summery, needs, call to action and hook. You need to practice it so that it flows, but doesn't sound rehearsed or canned.*

Chapter 7

Five-Minute Networking

Networking Tip: Ask what they need. Do not tell them what you think they need. Never assume for them – gather information for a realistic analysis.

Networking Tip: This is the introduction and education stage. Selling comes much later in the process.

Chapter7

Five-Minute Networking

When you network face to face, it's important to get in front of as many people in the room as possible. You have about five minutes per person to give your introduction and to learn enough about that person to determine if you want to start a business relationship. To be proactive and get the most out of those five minutes, implement these four steps: peek interest, ask the right questions, listen and educate — not sell.

Applying these four steps every time leads to networking success.

Step 1: Peek their interest. This is where your seven-word introduction comes into play. When you meet someone, you have seven seconds for that person to decide if he or she is interested in getting to know you better. If your seven-word sentence has that person saying *Hmmm, tell me more,* you may be on your way to a great connection. If he or she says

Huh? What is it you do? then you are probably not being clear and may have lost that person. It's important that your sentence is clear, honest, and makes people want to hear more.

I was at a networking event where I asked a man what he did and he said that he was a "profit engineer." I thought *Well that's catchy, but what does it mean?* What is does he do?

I felt as if I needed to play 20 Questions to find out what this man did. His lack of clarity caused me to lose interest.

If you are real estate agent and you only say *I am a real estate agent*, I might think to myself *I already know a bunch of real estate agents*. However, if instead you say *I help dreams come true through real estate*, I may think *Cool, I have dreams*. It is clear, catchy, creative and honest. People know exactly what you do.

Step 2: Ask the right questions. This is the most important part of this process. Have you ever seen the *Dating Game* on TV? They have only a few minutes and a couple of questions to get enough information about three people to see who they want to date. If they make the wrong decision, they must go on a weekend-long date with someone with whom they will be miserable. In networking, like in the

Dating Game, it's important to ask the right questions to learn the information you need.

Ask open-ended questions to encourage someone to tell you about his or her business. Also ask questions to find out if that person is your ideal client. I suggest these four questions to find out about someone's business.

1. What makes you different?
2. What do you do?
3. What do you need for your business in the next 60 days?
4. Who is your ideal client?

Please re-word these questions to sound like you. Be sincere, yet practiced — not canned.

Examples of how you might re-word these questions:

1. What sets you apart? There are a lot of agents, why should I use/refer you?
2. Please explain your services to me. What are the benefits of your products?
3. What can I do for you? Do you have any needs for which I may be able to refer someone to you?
4. We all need clients. What type of client are you looking for? Who could use your product and why?

Answer these four questions as if someone asked them of you. You'll find an exercise form on the next page to write these answers down. Be honest and thorough with your answers — nobody will see this form but you and this is a great exercise to make sure you get the information you need to access your best client.

If you are a website designer, and what makes you different is that you can design the best website in three days, you might ask *If you were having a new website designed, how long would you want it to take?* If you are a pet groomer and in the next 60 days you need three people who have pets and want to pamper them, your question might be as simple *as Do you have pets or know anyone who likes to spoil their pets?* You are asking questions that cover your needs as well as the other person's needs. Be sure to keep your answers short, sweet, honest and to the point. Be respectful of people's time. Five minutes is all you have!

Step 3: Listen. This is essential for a great conversation. Listen and listen intently. Really hear what others are saying to you. You have two ears and one month — listen twice as much as you talk.

Step 4: Educate, don't sell. When someone asks about your business, it may be tempting to go right into selling mode. Keep in mind that in networking, you teach — not sell. This helps build relationships. When you educate, you *help* people with their needs — not benefit from them.

Keep the following exercise as a script and practice tool. First, answer the four questions as if someone were asking you. The questions can be about business or personal. The more you know if someone fits your ideal client, the faster you can qualify this contact. Example: *If you are in wellness, you may want to find out how they exercise in spare time or with family.* Then, list four questions you would ask someone else.

It helps to role play with a friend. Remember, this is called *Five-Minute Networking* — set a timer for five minutes. That's two and a half minutes for each of you. Practice this until you can complete it within the time allotted. After the first time, critique each other and then try it two more times or until you both feel very comfortable.

5-Minute Networking

1. What makes you different? _____

_____

_____

2. Tell me what you do _____

_____

_____

3. What do you need for your business in the next 60 days? _____

_____

_____

4. Who is your ideal client? _____

_____

_____

List questions you can ask to qualify your ideal client. Use the samples above to create questions in your words, that apply to what kind of clients you are looking for.

1. _____

_____

2. _____

_____

3. _____

_____

4._____

_____

Practice the questions and track what works best.
List comments and results below.

Comments _____

_____

_____

_____

In review: Five minutes is the length of time you have to meet someone, learn information about him or her and share information about you. Determine if there is a connection, exchange business cards and move on. Aim to get in front of as many new people as you can.

Not everyone at the event is someone you are meeting for the first time, however the five-minute rule still applies. Say hello, touch base, review needs, set up a coffee meeting and still keep it within five minutes. Be respectful of everyone's time. If people are standing by you waiting their turn to talk to you, you need to include them in your conversation. Then move on to someone else and keep networking. It is easy to just visit with people you know. However to grow, you need to meet new people. Ask people you talk to if they know anyone else in the room that you should know and let them introduce you.

Be honest, to the point, have fun and enjoy networking.

Chapter 8

Let's Do Coffee

Networking Tip: When scheduling a coffee meeting to get to know each other better, set a time limit for the meeting up front.

Networking Tip: Consider meeting for coffee to get acquainted with someone new. What better way to get to know each other than just sitting down and having coffee together?

Chapter 8

Let's Do Coffee

What is a coffee meeting? Why do we have the coffee meeting? What should I expect at a coffee meeting? I hear these questions all the time. In this chapter, we will answer these questions and help you feel more comfortable with the coffee meeting and explain what to do and expect. (Coffee meeting also known as the one-on-one.)

When you meet someone at a networking event who you want to get to know better, the coffee meeting is a possible next step.

To set up this meeting, call your new contact or send the "*Glad I met you* email" (we will discuss follow-up in Chapter 9). By scheduling a coffee meeting, you are asking to learn more about this person and to share your information with him or her. This is not a sales call. It's a meeting to build the relationship. By communicating that you and your contact will be sharing information, he or she does not misinterpret that you are scheduling the meeting to buy or sell something.

You need to set expectations for this meeting. Set a time limit for the meeting (set a one-hour limit and stay to it). Schedule a convenient time and place for both of you. The person requesting the meeting is in charge of the meeting and needs to confirm, be the time keeper and keep the meeting flowing. The more you know about each other, the easier building a relationship becomes. Eventually, you may decide to do business with this person or to make a referral.

Would you ask someone to marry you on the second date? I don't think so. The same goes with networking. Do not try to close the sale on the second meeting. With that said, you need to be prepared with the right tools and materials to give people all the information they need to make a decision. You might not take it out of your briefcase, however you should have it ready just in case. Remember ASK – Always sell kindly. This isn't the time in the process to sell, but if someone are very excited or you want that person's product, be prepared.

Meeting for coffee is a relaxed, social way to share information without selling. Meeting at his or her office may result in distractions. Going somewhere else for coffee provides a place where you have each other's full attention. I strongly recommend that you treat this as an appointment — do not take phone calls or text messaging during the meeting.

You talk, listen, think, listen and be honest with each other. Let's break this down a little. I know it sounds easy, but it is how we talk, listen, think, listen that makes the coffee meeting effective.

- When it's your turn to talk, keep it clear and easy to understand. Don't use too many technical terms.

- Don't run on and on about every product or service you have, only that which pertains to the person with whom you are meeting.

- Listen to his or her wants and needs communicate what you have to offer.

- Think about what you need.

- Think about who you can refer.

- Think about what you can do for your contact.

- Ask questions you may have to gain a better understanding of what your contact does.

- Listen again for more information and for any concerns or issues.

- Take notes so that when you follow up after the meeting, you can be clear and on target.

While you are doing all of this, have fun. This is relationship building to get to the point where you know, like and trust each other.

This is an illustration I use in my workshops to show the networking or relationship building cycle.

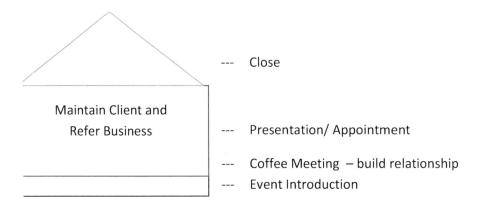

I have created a tool that helps you make the most of the coffee meeting or one-on-one. Below is a sample.

Coffee Appointment/One-on-One

Name _____Date_____

Company Name _____

Start Time ____ End Time ____ Location _____

Client Address _____

Phone # _____ Alternant Phone # _____
Best time to call _____

Email Address _____

Website _____

Questions _____

_____

_____

_____

_____

_____

_____

Notes _____

_____

_____

_____

_____

_____

_____

Next Step _____ -

_____

_____

_____

_____

Thank You Card _____ Appointment Date _____

Time _____ Confirmation _____

Location_____

Goal _____

Referral Given _____

Referral Received _____

Follow-Up _____

_____

_____

_____

_____

_____

Sample Questions

Please tell me a little about you.

Would you like to share with me why you do what you do?

What do you like to do for fun?

How long have you been in business?

What sets you apart from other like businesses (people)?

What do you need in the next 30 days?

Who is your ideal client?

Out of all your products/services, which is your favorite and why?

Do you know anyone who may be interested in using my services?

What can I do to help you personally or for your business?

Referral Questions

Do you know anyone who can benefit from my products/services? What is a great referral for you? What do you want me to share about you to a possible referral? Would you be willing to tell others about me?

Follow-up Tools

Contact management system (Outlook®, Neat Receipt®, Comf5®, Act®, Gold Mind®), card scanner, tracking system, email, phone calls, thank you cards, newsletters, postcards, social networking, video

Follow-up Notes _____

_____

_____

_____

_____

_____

_____

_____

Expectations and Goals _____

_____

_____

_____

_____

Testimonial _____

_____

_____

_____

In review: The coffee meeting takes place where you can get to know each other better after first meeting at a networking event. This is not a sales appointment. You are both only sharing and educating. This is the second step in building the relationship. Set expectations and a time limit. Have fun, yet stay on track. You want to have that *warm fuzzy* feeling.

Chapter 9

Follow Up, Follow Up, Follow Up

Networking Tip: Following up is more than just calling or sending an email the day after meeting someone new. It means getting invested to know a person.

Networking Tip: Follow up within the first 24 hours. Keep trying to make contact until the person says *stop*. Do what you say you will. If you say you will call back on Tuesday, call back on Tuesday.

Networking Tip: Do you find that you reach more voice mail in your follow-up than you do real people? Leave a message that peaks their interest and makes them want call you back immediately.

Chapter 9

Follow Up, Follow Up, Follow Up

Without the follow-up, networking is *just wine and meatballs*. This is the most important step and I will give you many tools and tips in this chapter for you to be more effective at following up.

In golf, it's called follow through, because you do it from the beginning of the swing. You need to hit through the ball from the start to the end of the swing. And follow this step until the ball is in the hole. This is also true in networking — from the first hand shake to the close of the business and through the relationship with the client. Follow-through is one continuous stroke. Envision the ball is moving down the fairway to the hole. Now envision a networking scenario. Imagine meeting someone at an event, sending a *"glad I met you* email," scheduling an appointment for coffee, sending a thank you card, meeting for coffee and so on until you close the business. Then you would continue following up to retain the business relationship. This is also known as the *sales cycle* or *building the relationship*.

Many people tell me that their biggest challenge with networking is the follow-up. They like going to meetings and events, yet find it hard to follow up and still have time to run their businesses.

Follow-up should happen within 24 hours. Why? The event and the conversation you had are fresh in your mind. There may be more than one person at the event in your field and they, too, may have spoken to this contact. Plus, the sooner you make contact, the sooner you can start building that business relationship. It is also easier to track and manage your time.

Let's break this down into doable steps. Here is a list of the tools and skills essential to good follow-up.

Tools	*Skills*
Calendar	Organization
Introduction	Relationship building
Time management	Contact manager system
Card scanner	Phone skills and scripts
Marketing materials	Persistence
Templates and scripts	Email System

Skills can be learned if you don't already have them. In my opinion, the most helpful skill is organization. You need to be organized to keep track of it all. You can take workshops, classes or read books — just educate yourself. A business coach or trainer can also help.

Let's look at each of the tools we need and how to use them for the best results.

Calendar. Block out time before and after events for follow-up. Plan for 10 to 15 minutes before an event and 10 minutes for every 30 minutes of networking. Treat events as appointments. When you have them on your calendar, you are less likely to break them. Set specific days of the week for coffee meetings or appointments. Google® has a good online calendar that can remind you of appointments. Plan out your time for business, fun and family.

Introduction. Know your introduction. Have it ready and practiced — not canned. It should be adaptable from 7 to 60 seconds long. Know the audience in the room so you can adapt your introduction to fit your audience.

Contact Manager System. Use this online system to organize your contacts and store their information. Find the one that works best for you. There are free systems or software you can purchase. There are even monthly programs. There's Outlook®, Act®, Goldmine® and Google®, just to name a few.

Card Scanner. Save time by scanning your cards into the computer and into the contact manager of your choice. A great card scanner is the NeatReceipt®. Not only does it scan business cards, but it also scans receipts and full sheets of paper. This is a good tool for networking and a great business tool. A smart phone is a good way to scan a card at the event if you want to make a referral or appointment on the spot.

Marketing Materials. Every business needs marketing materials such as brochures, business cards, flyers, post cards — whatever works best for you. All of your marketing materials should have a consistent look and message.

Templates and Scripts. Having templates and scripts for emails and phone calls makes follow-up easier and more effective. This helps you to be practiced — not canned.

Email Systems. There are many email systems available. Pick one that works best for you. I recommend one that has opt-in and opt-out options.

Never put people on your mailing list without their permission.

Using these tools and skills, let's create a system and follow-up strategy that works for everyone.

Your **calendar** should have all the events for the month on it as if they are appointments and schedule time before and after those events for follow-up and appointments. Remember to allow 10 to15 minutes of follow-up for every 30 minutes of networking. Using your calendar this way uses your **time management** skill. Set other appointments around events in the same area to keep you from going back and forth from one side of town to another.

You need to know what **marketing tools** to have with you at the event. So, before each event you need to know what type of event it is and which tools are applicable. (business cards, flyers, raffle prize, etc.). Know who is in the room by checking RSVP lists and talking to the registration desk and ambassadors. Know your products and introduction. Always carry extra marketing tools in the car just in case.

Within 24 hours after an event:
- **Scan** the business cards you acquired into your **contact management system**

- Call your new contacts to schedule appointments to meet with them or send them the *glad I met you* email. Use **templates and scripts** for speed, accuracy and consistency. If you get voice mail, leave a detailed message clearly stating what you want and need and set expectations.
- Follow up on voice mails and emails within three to four days. Continue trying to get in touch till they tell you to stop.

I recommend scheduling a casual **coffee meeting** to get to know each other better to see if this is a business fit. Follow these guidelines:
- Meet at a casual location.
- Clearly communicate that you want to learn about the other person. Share with him or her what you do so that both of you can determine if this is a business opportunity or a referral source.
- Set a time limit.
- Listen, be focused and be present.
- Remember this is not a sales appointment. It is a step in building the relationship.

If you make an appointment to meet after the coffee date, send a thank you note before your next appointment. This shows you care and reaffirms your upcoming appointment.

You can make your presentation at that next appointment. When you close the business deal, remember to ask for the referral. It's important to continue following up with your new clients in order to retain them. E-newsletters are great for staying in front of your prospects and clients.

The more organized you are, the easier and more effective a good follow-up system is for growing your business. Organize your products, tools and systems. If you need help, I recommend a business or organization coach. Coaches are great tools for business growth.

In review: The follow-up step is important to establish and use a system that works for you. The more you repeat this process, the better you will understand it. Without follow-up, networking is *just wine and meatballs*. Spend the time to build the relationship and ask for the business and the referral. Make those phone calls, send those emails and thank you cards, set those appointments and grow your business. Be creative in follow-up. Follow up after the introduction, the coffee meeting or next visit, the appointment, the close and throughout the relationship.

Chapter 10

Qualified Referral

Networking Tip: When you refer two people, keep in touch to see that they get together and it works. Follow up closely. People remember who referred them, rather than the bad or lack of service if it goes badly. It is very important to take your customer service the extra mile.

Networking Tip: Be specific about what you need and what client you want to help people give you better referrals.

Networking Tip: Giving referrals is like matchmaking. You need to know, like and trust both parties to put them together. It's more than a name and phone number.

Chapter 10

Qualified Referral

Asking for referrals may be the most feared and misunderstood part of networking. If you had to choose between one client for a lifetime or 10 people who refer you to 10 people who refer you, which would you chose for growing your business and keeping it growing? I think you'll agree that the answer is *10 people who refer you.* The question then is, *How can you get those people to be a part of your business on a regular basis?*

What is a qualified referral*?* For the purposed of this book, we will define *qualified referral* as*:*

A person or business recommended to someone who has the qualities or accomplishments to fit a needed function.

The main purpose of networking is to find qualified referrals. As networkers, we want to give and receive as many qualified referrals as possible in order to grow our businesses. Many successful sales people can ask for the order, yet find it extremely difficult to ask for the referral. In networking, we can ask for the referral even if someone hasn't purchased our product.

The best way to get referrals is to give referrals. What I want you to learn from this chapter is:

1. How to qualify a referral
2. How to ask for a referral
3. How to give a referral
4. Why you should follow up on referral

How to Ask for the Referral.

When someone asks for your business card and you hand that person two, you are asking for the referral from the beginning. Please understand that he or she needs to get to know you better before referring you. Still, your bold move shows your confidence. During your conversation, you can ask if that person knows anyone who may need or be interested in your service or product.

A great time to ask for a referral is after you have provided a service for someone. Within the first month, while the client is still in the honeymoon stage and very happy with your product or service, ask if your client knows someone who can benefit as he or she has. People love to share a great find with their friends. If you feel uncomfortable asking, you can make it part of your paperwork. While you're at it, include a request for referrals in all of your marketing tools including your business cards, brochures, post cards and emails.

How to Make it a *Qualified* Referral

To make it a *qualified* referral, talk to both parties to make sure that they are both interested in connecting with each other. Then help them make that connection. Stay in touch with them to make sure the connection works. If it turns out that they are not a fit for each other, make the effort to find someone else for your contact. If you set up a connection and one person doesn't follow through, you are right there to make sure the connection happens. If you find that a person you refer doesn't follow up, you may want to stop referring them or make sure you stay close throughout the transaction.

Ask a lot of questions. Make sure you know, like and trust both parties involved in the referral. Understand the needs and abilities of the parties you are referring. If someone *says I need a landscaper*, ask if he or she needs lawn care, design or tree removal. It is important to learn specific needs. The more you know the better you can help.

How to Give a Referral

Both parties you are connecting should expect the referral and feel the sense of urgency. If you only tell one of them, the connection may never happen. I suggest you call or email both parties to notify them and follow up on the results. I usually send an email saying something like, *Joe here is Sam's information*

I told you about. This email is copied to both of you. Please feel free to contact each other within 24 hours. I will follow up with you both next week Tuesday to see how it goes. Call me with any questions. Thank you. If you have a smart phone, you can give the information to each of the parties while still talking to them during an event. Whenever possible, introduce them in person. This adds to credibility and you know that the meeting has taken place.

It's worth repeating that it is important to follow up on a referral to make sure all went well. People get busy, lose the phone number or feel uncomfortable making the call. Conflicting personalities may come into play, therefore you may want to provide multiple names to one person to interview them all and pick the right fit.

If you give a referral and so does someone else, and the business goes to the other choice, let your friend know what happened.

Giving and receiving referrals is essential to growing business. Most importantly, your reputation is on the line. Follow up, ask the right questions to qualify and give a referral whenever you can. When you are networking, you may not be doing business with the people in the room, but with the people they know. Get to know, like and trust your friends and clients and you will be successful and blessed.

Be specific when asking or giving a referral. Example: You might say you are looking for women clients. I may know 100 women, so it would be difficult to come up with a name. If you say *I am looking for women between 25 and 30 years of age, who want to work out in the gym to stay fit and healthy*, one or two names may come to mind that I can share with you. People don't always get this. Therefore, I created this form to show you how to be specific and what to ask for to get and give the best qualified referrals. The more specific you, are the more qualified the referral. This form also works to know what to ask for from someone needing a referral to make sure you fit the exact needs.

The Best Referral

If you have more than one business or product, pick one for this exercise.

Business _____,

Product _____

Who is your ideal client _____

List 3 things that make them your ideal client.

_____
_____
_____

Number them by importance.

List three things you do for them (WIFM).

_____

_____

_____

Number them by importance.

List three Characteristics of your Ideal Client.

_____

_____

_____

Number them by importance.

Write down your Ideal client and the number one item from each list above.

_____

_____

_____

_____

_____

This is your ideal referral. Be specific.

In review: Referrals grow your business as well as your clients' businesses. If you help others grow, everyone can be successful. Ask for the referral every time. Know the specific needs of both parties to make sure you provide a good fit. *Qualify the referral.* Follow up to make sure each person received what he or she needed. The best way to get referrals is to give referrals.

People remember you for providing referrals. Your reputation is valuable. Giving referrals comes back to you five-fold.

Chapter 11

Networking for Life

(a job, dating, and more)

Networking Tip: Give more, Take less equals better results

Networking Tip: When you live your life giving to others, your life is so much better.

Chapter 11

Networking for Life

They should teach us networking skills as children. These are skills we can use throughout life. If we learn these skills early on, everything would be easier — high school would be less scary! Here are a few points in our lives in which good networking skills make a big difference.

1. **College.** Learn about the school and sell your achievements to the board for acceptance. Create a business card with your contact information and a couple of points of achievements.
2. **Dating.** Looking for that person with whom to spend the rest of your life. Networking skills help you know what you want and promote yourself honestly. They help you build a relationship, get to know the person and ask

the right questions. Create a business card with contact information, hobbies and interests.

3. **Job/Career.** Chambers and meet-up groups are good for networking for a job. You don't want to walk into a mixer with a stack of resumes and hand them out to everyone in the room. Create a business card with your contact information and a couple of bullet points about yourself — leave plenty of white space for people to write notes. Check the RSVP list and know who is in the room. Let as many people in the room know that you are looking for work and what kind of work you are looking for. Don't say *I am unemployed* and don't talk negatively about your previous employer. Say that you are in transition. Be positive, focused and precise as to what you are looking for. Realize that the people doing the hiring are most likely not there networking. However, you may meet people who know someone who is hiring. You may impress someone enough to refer you to a client or close friend who happens to be hiring. Ask permission to drop off or email your resume. Follow up with that person within 24 hours. With job hunting, persistence is a good thing. Follow up often. Check out job boards on chamber, meet-up and online social networking sites like LinkedIn® and Facebook®.

4. **Business.** Networking skills are valuable in any business scenario, whether you work for someone else, own your own business, want to start one or have a side business for a second income stream.

5. **Retirement.** Networking skills even help in this chapter in your life. You meet new people on vacation and follow up with them, meet people in assisted living centers, connect with people who can help you with the decisions you need to make after you retire.

These are a few points of networking. There are many more, but I think you get the idea. If we approach all the different aspects of our life with the idea of putting others first, helping others grow, sharing and educating with others, we could have a full and successful life. Teaching these skills to our children prepares them for life and business at an early age and gives them the head start they need.

As in networking for business, the most important thing to remember when networking for life is that it's about building relationships and following up. You need to stay in touch with the people in our life to continue to grow. You never know when knowing them will help with something you need. How many times in your life have you thought *It's a small world* when someone connected to the past becomes a very important part of your future.

In review: You need to practice and use networking skills in all aspects of your life. Be willing to help others, share and educate. Ask questions to get to know, like and trust the people in our lives. Keep in touch through follow-up.

Chapter 12

Building relationships

Networking Tip: Relationships should be built on a good foundation. Foundations are made of trust and integrity.

Networking Tip: When building business relationships, realize that not everyone is the perfect client. However, they may be a friend or referral source.

Chapter 12

Building Relationships

Building relationships is what networking is all about. I left this chapter as the last because I feel all the skills and tools we talked about in networking helps you to be better at building relationships. I wanted to give you tools to build and keep relationships.

When you start a dating relationship you don't typically ask someone to marry you on the first date. You get to know all you can about each other before you decide to make a commitment. It doesn't always become a committed relationship. Not everyone becomes your friend or life partner. Friendships come and go. The same works in business relationships, if you try to sell too soon you can hurt the relationship and make it harder to trust. Not everyone you meet is a client. Clients come and go.

If you follow a few simple steps you can build a good relationship. Use what you learn in this chapter to make friends, business relationships, acquaintances and referral partners.

Six Steps to Building a Relationship

We have gone through these steps in detail throughout the book and I will summarize them here:

1. **Introduction.** Make a good first impression. Keep your introduction honest, sincere and passionate — not salesy.
2. **Courtship.** This is your educating and learning through coffee meetings and communication via phone, email and thank you cards. Set expectations and start the relationship.
3. **Commitment.** This is the sale where you agree to do business or become friends, where your contact becomes your client and the maintenance part of the relationship begins. This is still the beginning of the relationship — you must work to continually learn and educate each other.
4. **Growth**. As you both grow and change, so does the relationship. You must continue to nurture and feed through communication. During this growth, ask for and give referrals on a regular basis.

5. **Let Go**. Not every relationship will be great for you or your business. Know when to end a relationship. Sometimes you have to fire your customer. This can be difficult, however you have to determine if the time and effort you're putting in is equal to what you are getting in return. If not, let the person go.
6. **Refer**. Share this relationship with others and encourage the other person to share you, too.

You need the same tools to build relationships as you do to be great at networking.

1. **Confidence.** Be honest and passionate. Have integrity and believe in your products and services.
2. **Systems.** Put the processes in place that you need in order to grow — goals, plans and outcomes.
3. **Organization.** Be very organized. Track your time, money and efforts.
4. **Communicate.** Keep in touch. Have a strong communication program in place. See the Client Relationship Checklist below.
5. **Time Management.** Be respectful of everyone's time. Once it's gone, you can't get it back.

6. **Reward.** Reward yourself, your vendors, your clients, your friends and your family. Say *thank you.*
7. **Refer.** This is both a step *and* a tool. It is the backbone of networking, building relationships and growing.

Let's take the list above and the things you learned throughout and put them into a system and checklist you can start using now to be more effective at building relationships.

I suggest you set up recognition programs in your business — one to reward your staff and one to reward your vendors and clients. This will allow you to recognize them for greatness help you to treat everyone equally. You will be more likely to follow through.

Here is a relationship building checklist to use as a guide.

Client Relationship Checklist

Client _____

Email _____

Phone _____ Phone 2 _____

Website _____

Address_____

Social Media	Phone call	Email	Thank you	Visit	Present ation	Reward	Referral	Lunch Dates

Record your actions with each and every client. You can make this form as simple or as advanced as you like. Leave space for dates and actions. Set a goal to see each client in person twice a month, have lunch together once a quarter. As you nurture these relationships, you may find the frequency may change more in the beginning and less as the relationship matures. Set up a similar system for employees.

Surveys and feedback are important parts of communication most people miss. From time to time, ask people what they like and dislike about your products and services. When you receive feedback, address it.

A rewards program is a great way to build and maintain great relationships and get more referrals. Have special events for all your clients, give rewards for long-time valued clients and for most referrals.

Host holiday parties and company picnics. Reward clients, staff and family. Everyone appreciates a pat on the back.

We have shown you where you can network and how to create an adaptable introduction. We taught you the questions to ask and gave you the follow-up tools. We shared the dos and don'ts. It's now up to you to put it together, practice it, work it and perfect it. You can do it! Networking should not be feared. We have been doing it all our lives. Remember, this is only one way to market your business. You need to use all five types of marketing to be successful. The five types of marketing are:

1. Advertising

2. Networking

3. Promotion

4. Public relations

5. Customer service

I feel networking should be a way of life, always putting others' wants and needs above our own. Imagine what a great place this could be if we all did this. Be good humans and please give all you got.

In review: The seven tools to relationship building are confidence, systems, organization, communication, time management, reward and referrals. Networking is all about relationship building and follow-up. Networking is one fifth of your marketing plan.

Chapter 13

Review:
To Be the Effective Networker

Networking Tip: Be prepared, present, focused, ask for the referral and always follow up.

Networking Tip: It's not about you. Share, educate, build the relationship through giving and receiving referrals.

Chapter 13
Review
To Be the Effective Networker

Networking has been a part of business and our lives for a very long time. We can be very successful using networking skills and tools effectively. Let's review what is in this book.

Where to Network: Chambers of commerce, associations, lead source groups, meet up/mastermind, service organizations and even toastmasters. You need to check them out before joining. Go online and visit their meetings. Use the three/three rule and be sure you have the warm and fuzzy feeling with the group.

Swing into Networking: Networking is like golf — you need to have the right tools, skills, passion, a strong work ethic and practice. The important part of golf is the follow through. The important part of networking is the follow-up.

Three Key Strategies to Better Networking:
Remember to prepare like it's an appointment, know who is in the room and have the proper tools. Have a plan and stick to it. Stay focused. Finally, set doable goals and share them with others.

The Six Characters of Networking and what we can do instead.

1. *The Card Player* passes business cards to and receives business cards from everyone. Instead, only give and receive requested cards — and only when you have talked with the person.
2. *The Magician* adds people to his or her mailing list without permission. Instead, ask permission to email and get to know people first.
3. *The Badge Gazer* reads badges and only talks to people in a certain industry. Instead, meet everyone regardless of industry. You don't know who may have the Verizon network behind them, and can introduce you to the person who becomes your next big client.
4. *The Closer* pounces on you and tries to sell at events. Instead, know the importance of a good

introduction. Educate people without selling to them. Remember that it's not about you and that the selling takes place at a later time.

5. **The Town Crier** talks all about himself or herself, wanting to be the center of attention. This person has the best product or service there is and knows everything and then some. Instead, listen and share. Be honest, have integrity and be sincere.

6. **The Crasher** interrupts conversations. Instead, wait to be invited into the conversation.

Just be *you*, have fun and ASK — always sell kindly.

Adaptable Introduction: The introduction is a significant part of networking. By making it adaptable, we have our seven-second introduction that opens up the lines of communication. The 30- to 60-second introduction tells our story. It has 5 parts: introduction, summery, needs, call to action and the hook. Practice it so it flows, but doesn't sound rehearsed or canned.

Five-Minute Networking: Five minutes is the length of time you have to meet someone, learn information about him or her and share information about you. Determine if there is a connection, exchange business cards and move on. Aim to get in front of as many new people you can.

Not everyone at the event is someone you are meeting for the first time, however the five-minute rule still applies. Say hello, touch base, review needs, set up a coffee meeting and still keep it within five minutes. Be respectful of everyone's time. If people start standing by you waiting their turn to talk to you, you need to include them in your conversation. Then move on to someone else and keep networking. It's easy to just visit with people you know. However to grow, you need to meet new people. Ask the person you are talking to if he or she knows anyone else in the room you should know and let them introduce you.

Be honest, to the point, have fun and enjoy networking.

Let's Do Coffee: The coffee meeting takes place where you can get to know each other better after first meeting at a networking event. This is not a sales appointment. You are both only sharing and educating. This is the second step in building the relationship. Set expectations and a time limit. Have fun, yet stay on track. You want to have that *warm fuzzy* feeling.

Follow-Up, Follow-up, Follow-up: The follow-up step is important to establish and use a system that works for you. The more you repeat this process, the better you will understand it. Without follow-up, networking is *just wine and meatballs*. Spend the time to build the relationship and ask for the business and the referral. Make those phone calls, send those emails, thank you cards, set those appointments and grow your business. Be creative in follow-up. You follow up after the introduction, coffee meeting or next visit, the appointment, the close and throughout the relationship.

Qualified Referral — Referrals grow your business as well as your clients' businesses. If you help others grow, everyone can be successful. Ask for the referral every time. Know the specific needs of both parties to make sure you provide a good fit. *Qualify the referral.* Follow up to make sure each person received what he or she needed. The best way to get referrals is to give referrals. People remember you for providing referrals. Your reputation is valuable. Giving referrals comes back to you fivefold.

Networking for Life — Networking skills needs to practiced and used in all aspects of our life. Be willing to help others, share and educate. Ask questions to get to know, like and trust the people in our lives. Keep in touch through follow up.

Relationship Building — review The seven tools to relationship building is, confidence, systems, organization, communication, time management, reward, and referrals. Networking is all about relationship building and follow-up. Networking is one fifth of your marketing plan.

Websites

www.itsmorethanwineandmeatball.com.

www.jordansreferralnetwork.com

http://www.facebook.com/janice.jordan.94

http://www.facebook.com/jordansreferralnetwork

http://www.facebook.com/wineandmeatballs

http://www.linkedin.com/in/janicejordan

A workbook with all the forms, exercises and tracking forms is available.

Thank you for reading and please share this book with others. *Happy networking.*

ABOUT THE AUTHOR

Janice Jordan - Speaker, Trainer, Coach, Author

Janice Jordan is a dynamic speaker with a wealth of knowledge about networking. For the past 25 years, she has had a highly unconventional career path, including sales at Xerox, Val Pak and Penney Saver, and being entrepreneur. She has owned numerous successful businesses. Janice was number one in sales using her networking skills and cold calling to get new clients. Well known as a networking coach and trainer with her current company, Jordan's Referral Network, Janice is considered an expert in relationship building and connecting the right people. She shows business leaders how to get the most out of their networking efforts and how to get a referral every time.

When Janice realized that networking and teaching networking was her passion, she researched and studied all she could about chambers of commerce, networking groups and organizations. Then she studied people and what they were doing. After reading many books, Janice decided that what today's business people need is a guide with tools to quickly get them where they want to be.

Janice participates both face to face and online in many chambers of commerce and various networking groups. She has been called the Network Queen because she is willing to share her wealth of knowledge with everyone she can. She walks and talks networking.